THE BEATLES
In the Beginning

THE BEATLES
In the Beginning

Photographs and Text by

HARRY BENSON

UNIVERSE

Who else could I dedicate the book to but my family — Gigi, Tessa, and Wendy

Acknowledgments

I WOULD LIKE TO THANK Derek Taylor for introducing me to the Beatles; Frank Spooner for giving me the assignment to photograph them; and the Beatles for the privilege of photographing them. I would also like to thank the picture editors who have always been there for me: M. C. Marden, David Friend, Susan Vermazen, and John Loengard; photographers David Cairns and Jon Delano; and especially my editor on this book, Manuela Soares, for her patience, enthusiasm, and guidance; and lastly, my wife, Gigi, and my mother, Mary, for always believing in me.

Previous page: The Beatles were coming out of the shadows to go on at the Boston racetrack during the third world tour in 1966. When the audience caught a glimpse of them, the noise of the crowd became deafening.

Published by
Universe
300 Park Avenue South
New York, NY 10010

© 1993 Harry Benson, Ltd.
All rights reserved

Design by Douglas & Voss Group, New York

Printed in Hong Kong

Contents

This photo of me with Paul, George, and Ringo was taken by John Lennon with my camera at the George V in Paris at about two in the morning. "Now it's your turn, Harry," he said. They had just finished a show at the Olympia.

Introduction

The FIRST TIME I met the Beatles was on their first trip to Paris. There had been another London newspaper photographer on the assignment in England, but the Beatles didn't like him because he was ugly; the worst thing you could be around the Beatles was ugly.

There was a Manchester newspaper reporter called Derek Taylor whom the Beatles liked and trusted. Derek was a superb journalist. If it hadn't been for Derek, I wouldn't have moved an inch with the Beatles. He was the one who sent me to meet them and they liked me, so I got the assignment to travel with them and photograph them. At first I didn't know enough about that kind of music. I was much more into Sammy Davis, Jr., Johnny Mathis, and Frank Sinatra.

The first time I heard them play was in a little place on the outskirts of Paris (not at the Olympia, where they played later in the week). I photographed them first backstage. When I went to take a picture from the front of the stage, they started singing "All My Loving" and I really thought it was wonderful. It was the first song I heard and it will always be my definitive Beatles song.

When they went out to this little gig on the outskirts of Paris, I remember Paul McCartney saying something like, "This is our first trip to Paris, give us your support." But they didn't need any, they took the audience by storm.

The press loved the Beatles. They were enormously talented, always a good story, arguably the most popular group ever. Before I met them in Paris I didn't really care if I did the story or not, but when I heard the music I changed my mind. It didn't take long to figure out that they were a phenomenon. Looking back on my career, some stories I'd love to go back and do again, but not the Beatles. I know I covered them to the best of my ability.

I remember George Harrison used to say he never expected to make any money with the band — just enough to open a little business. Six, seven months, that's what he thought it would be because rock groups come and go so quickly, replaced by other rock performers. George had bought a Jaguar XK-140 and was hoping that he would be able to make enough money to keep it, maybe by doing shows himself. Ringo Starr wanted to open a hair dresser's. They weren't sure it was going to last. Supremely confident, John said he always felt success was just a matter of time. Paul, ever aware of their image, was determined to get ahead.

What was funny about the Beatles was that, at the beginning, everyone around them was such a "great guy." As time passed, they began to see that people had ulterior motives for wanting to be with them. In the beginning they were really exploited, not just by the people you'd expect, people wanting concessions — Beatles hats, t-shirts, and such — but by the British aristocracy, who wanted them at their parties. I can honestly say that my only interest in them was to get more exclusive pictures for my newspaper before my competitors, the other British dailies, got theirs. It worked both ways, the Beatles got the publicity and I got the pictures.

Brian Epstein, their manager, was the least manipulative manager I've ever seen. He never really stopped anyone from getting to the Beatles for an interview, which meant that there was always a lot of publicity for them and that was important in the early days.

I saw changes in them in the three or so years that I covered their tours. I saw them become more sophisticated, more jaded, yet they were always witty, always quick. The whole world opened up to them and wanted to meet them.

The Beatles not only changed the world, they changed my life as well. I would never have gotten out of Britain, never been any kind of photographer if by chance I hadn't photographed the Beatles. Of course it changed my life; I came to America with them and never went back. You can't change your life any more than that.

Composing

I WAS IN THE SITTING ROOM of their suite in the George V Hotel in Paris. It was late afternoon. It wasn't time to get ready for the show that night, but they didn't have enough time to go out. First Ringo came in and sat down at the piano. Then Paul came in and was joined by John. Ringo knew to get out of their way, and he just slipped into the background as Paul and John sat down at the piano and started playing a few notes.

Harrison came over with his guitar and began playing a few bars, helping them with the song. They were completely into it. They knew what they were doing. They weren't just playing about. They were very intense, completely absorbed in what they were doing. This went on for hours. I had become invisible. They were so intent on what they were doing that they completely lost track of the time. You could feel the creative energy in the room.

I am pleased with these pictures because there are not many photographs of the Beatles actually composing. Afterward, they had food sent up and then went to do the show at the Olympia. They ordered a lot of room service. When they were in their rooms, not able to go out because of the crowds, they would order a bottle of Scotch, Chivas Regal. There might even be a bottle of Chivas Regal at the other

end of the room, but they just didn't want to get up and get it. They liked the idea of being able to call up and order anything they wanted. This ability to spend money, that's what they liked. Spending money gave them something to do with the idle time in their rooms. There would be trolley after trolley of food just lying around. They would taste it and go on to the next thing; the waste was just terrible. They had come so far so quickly. They were just kids from Liverpool and now they had all this. Not bad at all.

The composers I have seen usually just sit by the piano pinging away on the keys. At first, nothing much makes sense, but familiar strains soon start coming through. How quickly the Beatles got completely engrossed, oblivious to my presence. They had already written a lot of great music, hits like "She Loves You," " Love Me Do," and "I Want to Hold Your Hand." They always said how much American musicians influenced them, especially Buddy Holly.

As they played, I heard the melody first and then the words, "My baby's good to me, you know, she buys me diamond rings, you know." I'm pleased I photographed them composing "I Feel Fine."

Both McCartney and Lennon had very strong egos, very strong personalities, yet they respected one another.

That is one reason why they wrote great music together. Lennon and McCartney are arguably the two most famous composers in the history of music. Epstein told me that the money was being split four ways equally, except that the royalties for writing the songs went to the ones who wrote them — mainly John and Paul. Although George was writing, too, and even started his own music publishing business later that year, John and Paul dominated the music.

Of the four of them, George had the hardest time. Ringo knew he was lucky to be there. George had talent but was left out of the loop so to speak. They didn't particularly like his music and George resented it. I also think he felt a bit stifled creatively. He kept them right musically and he was probably the best guitar player among them.

When the Beatles first started back in Liverpool, they had another drummer, Pete Best, whom they later fired. One night at dinner Lennon mentioned why they had gotten rid of Best; he said it was because of Best's mother. Supposedly she was trying to take over the Beatles. Lennon said that's "the truth." She was trying to run the Beatles her way. Pete Best was obviously a touchy name to bring up with the Beatles. Think about it, this guy would have been a multi-millionaire. He was one of the originals and they just cut him right out.

I know that Brian Epstein, their manager, did not like how they handled it at all. He didn't like what happened to Best; he would rather not have had to replace him, but Epstein never got in the way, never tried to force his opinion on the group. He never tried to control the group and that was very important. But he was the one who had to tell Pete that the other boys wanted him out of the group.

When I asked about Ringo, Epstein said, "He's better than I expected." Epstein admitted he had been very worried about how Ringo would do and he was surprised and pleased at how well he fit in.

Here are a few of the songs the
Beatles recorded in 1964:

"One and One Is Two"

"You Can't Do That"

"I Should Have Known Better"

"And I Love Her"

"Tell Me Why"

"If I Fell"

"I'm Happy Just to Dance With You"

"Long Tall Sally"

"I Call Your Name"

"I'll Cry Instead"

"I'll Be Back"

"Matchbox"

"Slow Down"

"Anytime At All"

"Things We Said Today"

"When I Get Home"

"I'm A Loser"

"Mr. Moonlight"

"No Reply"

"Every Little Thing"

"Eight Days A Week"

"She's A Woman"

"I Feel Fine"

"Kansas City"

"Hey Hey Hey Hey"

"I'll Follow the Sun"

"Everybody's Trying to be My Baby"

"Rock and Roll Music"

"Words of Love"

"Honey Don't"

"What You're Doing"

Paris

THEY WENT SIGHTSEEING on the Champs Elysées, which was not more than 100 yards or so from their hotel, the exclusive George V. I wanted to get a picture of them on the streets of Paris, but it was so hard to go anywhere because of the fans and because it is hard to get four people organized at the same time. Three would be waiting in the car for the fourth and everybody would get restless and one would go back into the hotel to get the fourth and then the fourth would come out and the other one would be inside looking for him. Things like that went on all the time.

It was a cold day for sightseeing, but we went anyway. John and Paul had vacationed together in Paris a couple of years before and knew a bit about the city. We didn't go far because there were too many people about. They liked playing tourist and seeing a few of the sights, even if most of them were only on the postcards. The Beatles all had cameras and they all liked taking pictures, even if it was only of each other.

The French were blasé, trying hard not to pay too much attention to the Beatles. There were not many smiles on their faces, which is not unusual. It was also not unusual for someone to make a disparaging remark as they walked by. The Beatles just ignored them. Occasionally Lennon would answer back sharply, as he did once to a man walking his dog who was very rude and told them to go back where they came from. Lennon had had enough of such remarks and answered him with a stinging retort.

21

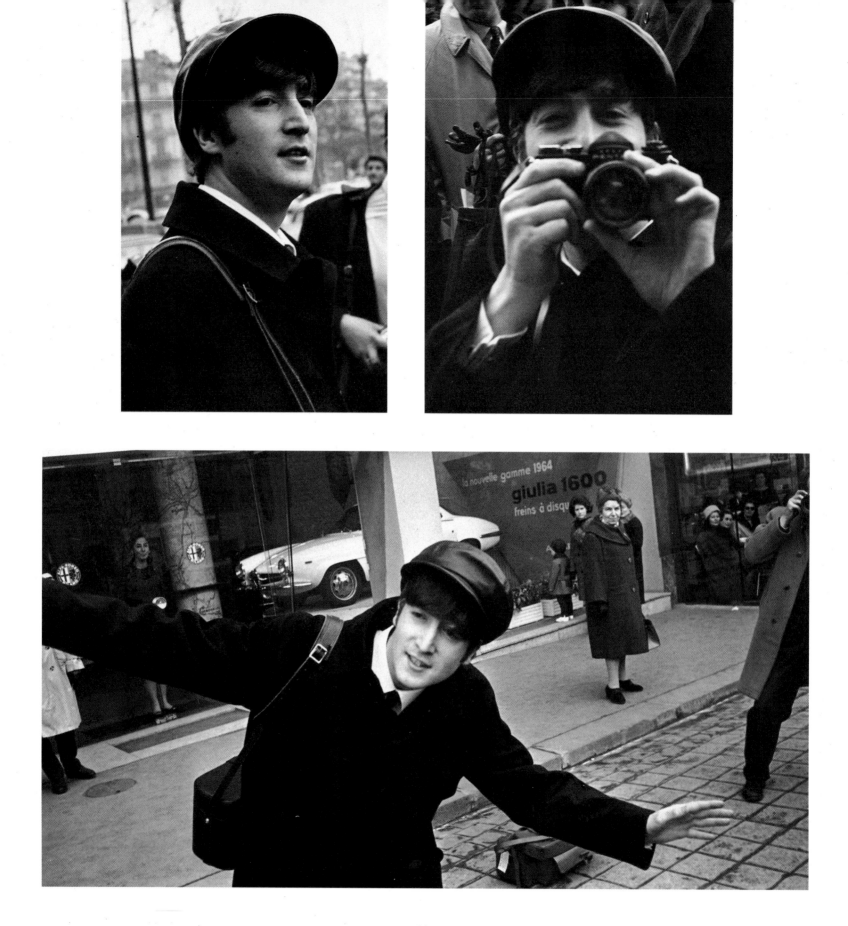

The Beatles were always smoking; they all smoked. They called them ciggies or fags (which is the British term for cigarettes). Later, of course, they all probably stopped, but back then everybody smoked.

When they landed at the Paris airport, there was a uniformed policeman or soldier standing there. He was very serious, intent on doing his job. The Beatles began clowning around and saluted him and he saluted back. They were carefree and always having fun, sending up authority in a light-hearted way. I think that part of the rea-

son they were so appealing is they were what everyone wanted to be — young, witty, carefree, and full of talent. But the main thing about them was that their music was so great; it touched all quarters of life.

Napoleon

ONE OF THE WAITERS said to Lennon in broken English that Lennon reminded him of the Napoleon bust in the lobby of the hotel, the George V. I personally didn't think that Lennon looked the least bit like him but sure enough, when we all went to the hotel lobby to see the bust of Napoleon on the way to the Olympia that night, they all stopped and thought John in fact did resemble it. I was joking, saying Napoleon would have been the fifth Beatle.

At the time Paul was considered the best looking Beatle, but I thought John was — he had a refined nose, an uncommon face. Anyway, I photographed Lennon in front of the bust of Napoleon and the rest of them lined up. I was looking for pictures no one else had. There is a limit to what you can do in a hotel room and still make a picture

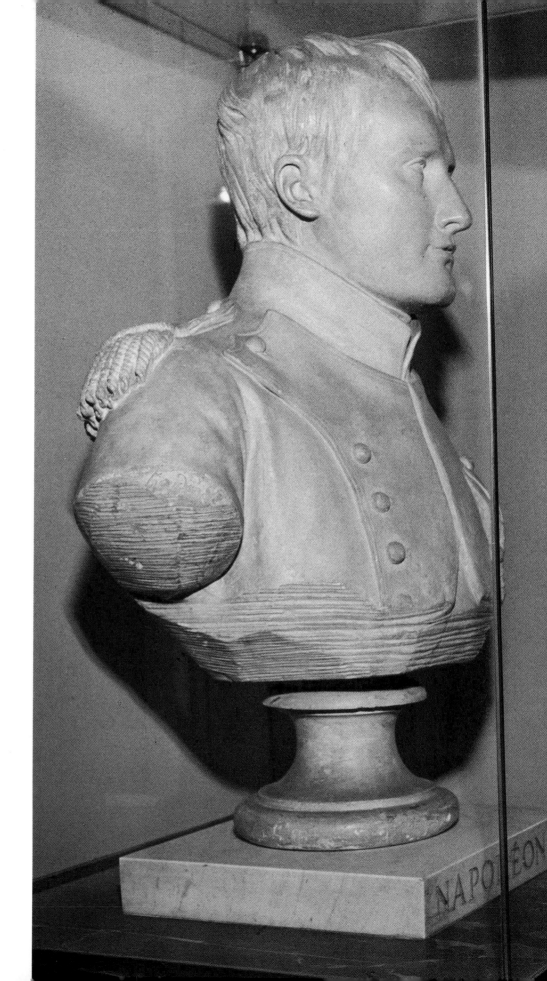

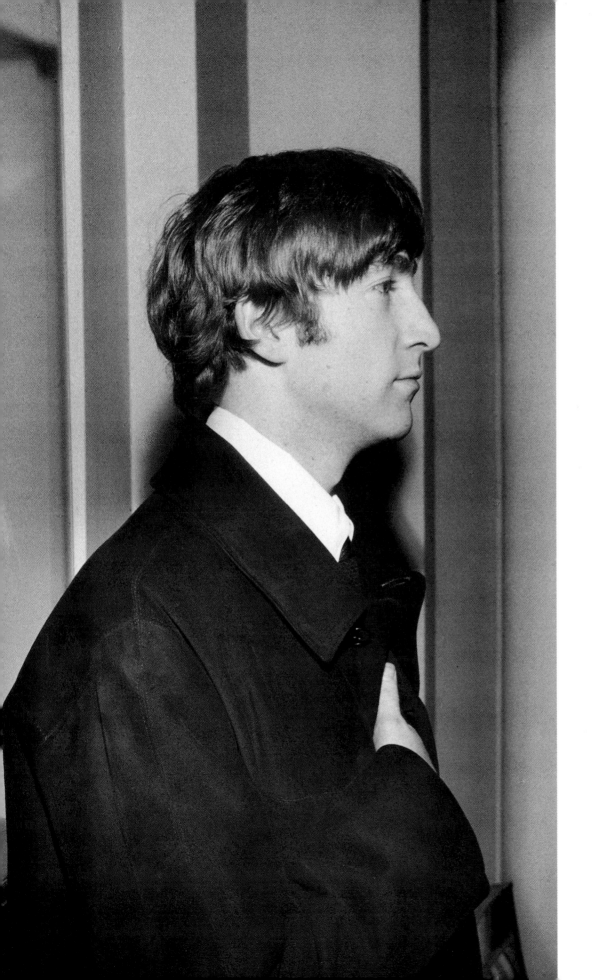

interesting. There were a lot of other photographers around who were also looking for different photos of the Beatles for their newspapers and magazines.

The Olympia

WE WERE ON OUR WAY to the Olympia for the evening's performance on opening night. I wanted to get a photo before they went onstage and the best I could do was to get them all in a bar near the Olympia on the rue de la Paix. The murals and posters on the wall looked typically French and made a good backdrop. It would also place them in Paris for the newspaper. They already had their make-up on and were ready to go on. We stopped in very quickly for something to drink and then raced over to the Olympia and around to the back door.

I remember that night in particular because there was a French photographer from the magazine *Paris Match*, I think, at the Olympia trying to get into the Beatles' dressing room. When they ran back into the Olympia, this overzealous French photographer was involved in a fracas with the French police who were

trying to keep order inside. Things were orderly outside the Olympia where the gendarmes were lined up, but inside it was another matter. The French photographer was being told to leave. The French photographers are a tough bunch, and you can bet he didn't leave without putting up a fight.

There were often fights around the Beatles. They had bodyguards, but I don't know how good they were. Mal Evans, a big, docile man, was in charge of the Beatles' security. Although they were accessible to all journalists and photographers, there had to be some semblance of order before they went on for their opening performance.

Trini Lopez and Sylvie Vartan were the two opening acts for the Beatles at the Olympia. It was rumored that Lopez hated their music. The Beatles were suspicious of Lopez's band because when they went on, two guitars wouldn't work and the electricity was messed up. There was a lot of chaos and carrying on as they tried to get all of the equipment ready before the performance. Needless to say the Beatles were very upset.

Gendarmes outside the Olympia.

Onstage

BRIAN EPSTEIN GAVE THEM THE IDEA to dress alike. He wanted them to look nice and clean-cut. I know that Lennon was dead against it because he used to make comments about them being in monkey suits. They had several different suits, but they were not nice looking at all. They were not well-made and looked kind of cheap up close, although they looked fine at a distance from the stage. Later, of course, they had some money to spend on clothes.

The Beatles always bowed after every song. At the gig outside Paris, and at the Olympia, they did their deep bow. Epstein told them to bow from the waist, but they didn't like it. Later, they stopped doing it. They were very different from the Elvis Presley kind of filling station sexiness. The Beatles appealed to all classes. They went right through the social strata from top to bottom. That was what made them so unique; the fact that they appealed to everybody. They were very presentable.

Beatlemania was starting to grow. It was Derek Taylor, the correspondent from Manchester, who I believe coined the word "Beatlemania." He later became the Beatles road manager.

When the Beatles' music was played in a bar or pub people would get up and dance to it. People who were doing a slow waltz a week ago were now dancing in a completely new way. Everything changed. It was a phenomenon. People changed their hair, their clothes. Everyone wanted to be a Beatle.

It's amazing to me the way people groveled to the Beatles all the time. Kings of exotic foreign

countries were always asking if they could come to meet them.

Although they were always very generous and hospitable, the Beatles were beginning to like this new found celebrity.

Lots of people even began copying how they spoke. People from the middle and upper classes in England started speaking with ridiculous Liverpool street accents because of the Beatles. People wanted to be like them. It was becoming infectious. Ironically, it was only around strangers or lots of people that they seemed to speak in a broader Liverpool accent. When you were alone with them, the accent was much less pronounced. Brian Epstein, of course, always spoke with a refined British accent.

The first time I met Epstein was in Paris. I liked him because he was so open, he didn't try to control or smother the Beatles. He didn't hold any of the press back from them in the early days, and that was vital. He was a man I would have liked to have said good bye to. The end of their touring in 1966 left Brian sad, without focus, and with nothing to organize or orchestrate. He wasn't needed in the recording studio like he had been on the tours. He died of an accidental overdose of sleeping pills in August 1967.

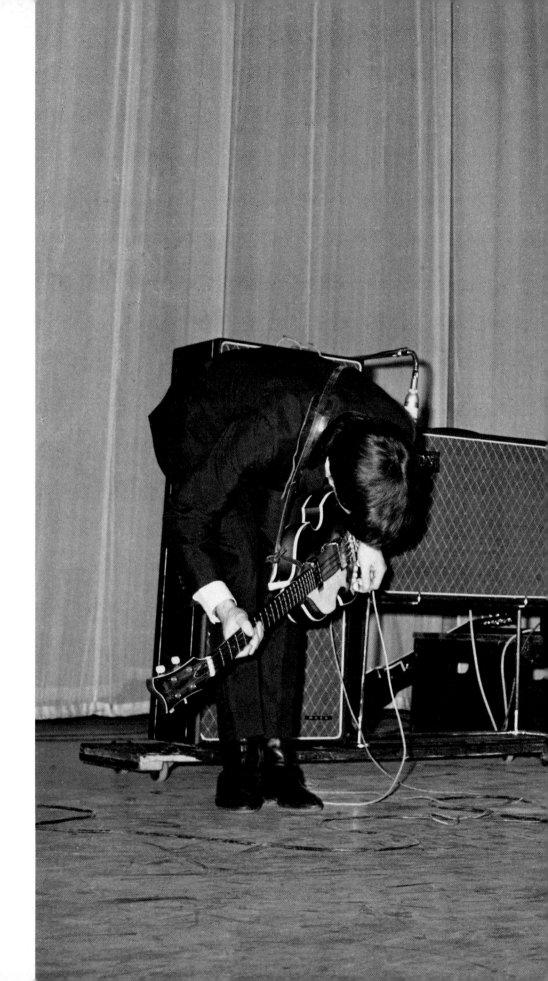

Fan Mail

THEY HAD JUST GOTTEN UP when this picture was taken, about three or four in the afternoon. A huge pile of fan mail had just arrived. They all sat around going through the letters and the packages addressed to each of them. John was the best looking one in the classic sense, but I think I would have a lot of women arguing with me on that. Paul had a cute little face. And George was nice looking, too. But, Ringo I believe, received the most fan mail. I think it was because he was the one they could get to. Women seemed to think their chances were better with Ringo. It had to be that.

Fans sent them a lot of presents, too. If someone sent three of one thing and there wasn't a fourth, the Beatle that was left out would sulk. They could get terribly peeved and upset. It was really very embarrassing to be in the room when they all got their presents from fans because they would fight and argue. A lot of the presents were cheap and silly things, idiotic rubbish like plastic swords, whistles, scarves, games to play on the plane, or girls' pictures, for instance. But if there weren't four of them, the excluded Beatle would go crazy. They would be grabbing things from one another, fighting over the toys. They were competitive over everything: women, attention, toys.

I know they actually called some girls after reading their letters. They would act cool like it was nothing, but I saw them going back to their bedrooms with letters in their pockets. The letters they read were the ones that had pictures of beautiful girls enclosed. A photograph was very, very important. If there was no photo, the letter was tossed aside.

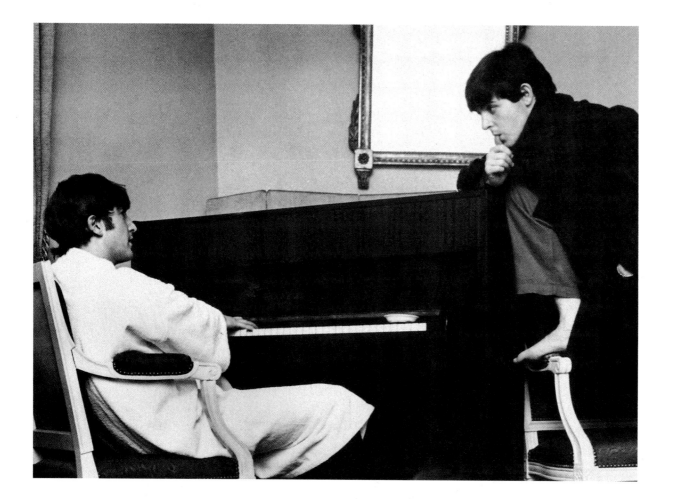

They usually opened these gifts at mealtime. They were always ordering room service — everything expensive — but in all the time I spent with them I never saw any drugs, although other writers were beginning to make hints at it. I saw plenty of booze though.

As the tour went on there were more and more fans at each stop. Fan reaction to the Beatles was always amazing. Even in Paris, where they weren't very well-known at the time, people reacted hysterically. At the Olympia, which reminded me of an old-fashioned village hall, every performance was sold out. As soon as the curtain went up and the Beatles began to sing, the kids started screaming, although I remember that there were a few stone-faced French couples in the audience, too, obviously hating every minute. But it was only the beginning for the Beatles and nothing was going to stop them.

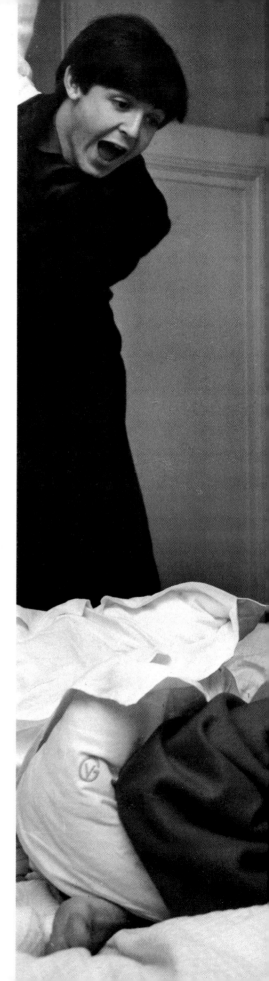

Pillow fight

ONE OF THE BEATLES — George, I think — was on the phone to some fan who managed to get a call through to them, and John hit him with a pillow. I said, "Do you do this often?" and they said, "All the time." But I waited and didn't do anything about it at the time. I waited for the right moment and it came a few days later. After one of the Paris shows at the Olympia, Epstein came in at 3 AM to tell them "I Want to Hold Your Hand" was the number one song in America and that they would be going there for the Ed Sullivan Show and their first American tour. When Epstein left the room I knew it was time. I said, "How about a pillow fight?"

They were caged up after each of the performances they gave at the Olympia, so there was a violent energy in them — this tremendous energy that had to be let out. They needed a way to let off steam. Security was very tight — Epstein especially was watching for any 13-year-old girls who might try and find their way into a Beatle's room.

I waited until I had them alone with no other photographers around. That's why I had stayed around until 3 in the morning — I wanted to make sure their own photographer, Dezo Hoffmann, was not there. I didn't want to give him any ideas. I never even told my reporter — "the Beatles might have a pillow fight" — I didn't want it written about before I photographed it.

The pillow fight became quite rough. They all seemed to take pleasure in hitting Paul. Paul was acting a bit superior so they really enjoyed giving it to him and he definitely got the worst of it. They all really enjoyed it. It was quite funny and it went on for a long time because they were enjoying it so much. They were so excited and happy about coming to America.

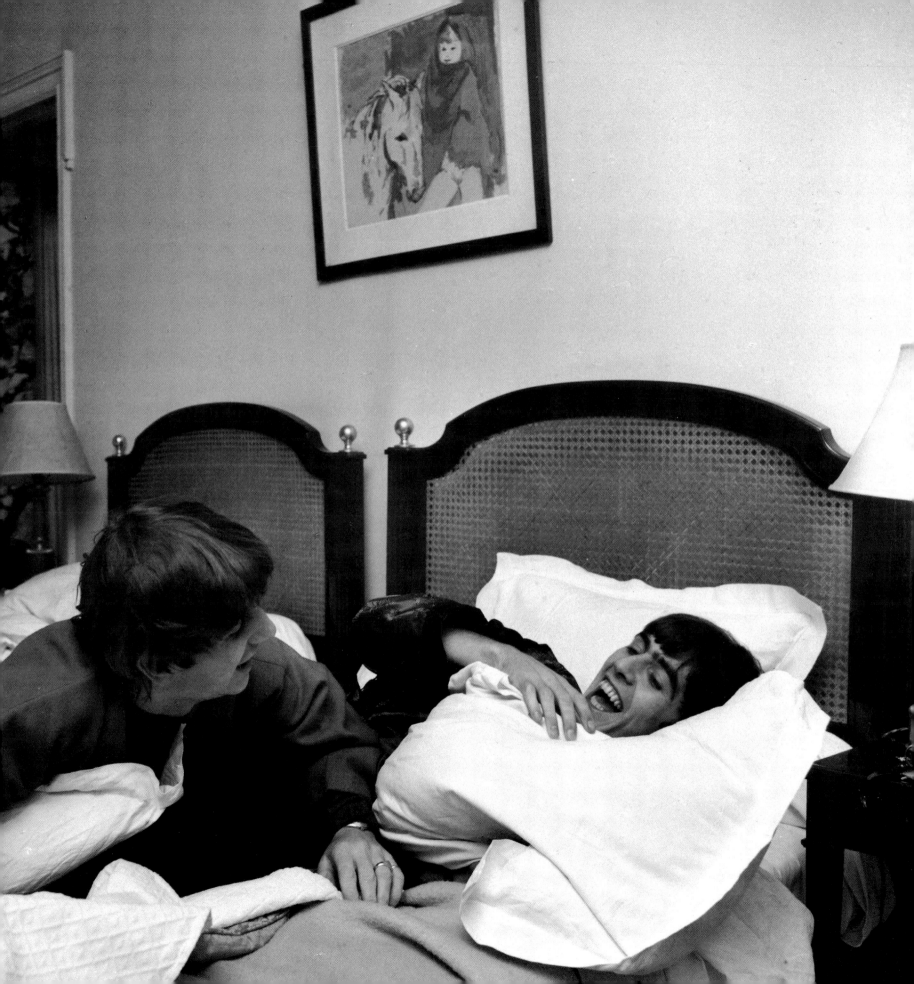

The pillow fight was in Paul and George's room and Paul said, "Why can't you do this in someone else's bedroom for a change?" The beds were a complete mess — all the sheets and blankets were pulled off. And in the middle of the night, there was no one around to remake them. I remember John was wearing navy blue pajamas and Ringo and Paul and George all wore red.

Jumping up and down on those fancy beds, spilling food and liquor on the rugs, you can see why rock groups are not invited back to the best hotels. It became a nightmare for housekeeping and for the security guards who were trying to keep the young girls out of the halls and elevators and lobby of the hotel. The fans would steal anything the Beatles had touched trying to get a souvenir of their idols. I even had my laundry stolen from the Plaza Hotel in New York because someone thought it belonged to George Harrison. We were sharing a suite and I sent my laundry out and it never came back.

What I have to thank for the pillow fight picture is my wide angle Rolleiflex with a powerful strobe on the camera. I managed to bounce the light off the ceiling. There's no way I could do this picture alone today without an assistant.

The Beatles really didn't take many things seriously in the beginning. They took any complaints or criticism very lightly, with a pinch of salt, so nothing became a problem. They were really quite thick-skinned. Once, at a press conference, reporters kept shouting questions and interrupting what the Beatles were trying to say. Brian Summerville, their road manager, shouted out, "Shut up! Would you all just shut up!" That stunned the audience — the press — and afterward a group of journalists told the Beatles that that kind of treatment of the press wouldn't do them any good. The Beatles listened, taking it all in, while the journalists somewhat pompously explained how that kind of rudeness could do the Beatles harm. Then George said, "Let Brian say what he likes. If anyone asks us about him, we'll just say we know he's daft." And everyone laughed. A potential problem, made light of, disappeared.

ON THE PLANE coming to America for the first time, John Lennon brought his first wife, Cynthia (Julian's mom). John and Cynthia were really quite quiet on the plane. I wondered what effect having Cynthia along would have on the fans' reception. I remember Brian Epstein being asked that question and saying something to the effect that the Beatles could do what they liked — he wasn't going to impose rules to tie them down, and John was entitled to bring his wife whenever he wanted. I remember Cynthia wore a black wig on the train ride from New York to Washington so that she wouldn't be recognized and stopped by the fans.

On the plane, Lennon was complaining about the British paparazzi who a few days earlier had sneaked up on them and taken a picture of their baby, Julian. Lennon was annoyed by that. To me it was just the beginning of what was going to become his life.

To pass the time, they took turns photographing each other. They all had cameras and loved to take pictures. In one photo Brian Epstein (seated) is talking to record producer Phil Spector. Paul was trying to sleep on the plane so he put a napkin over his head. He had been out very late the night before with model/actress Jane Asher, who was his girlfriend at the time.

There wasn't a reporter from my newspaper on the plane coming over to America with me, but I was met at the airport by

Andy Fyall from the New York office. Before we landed Lennon looked out of the window and said he didn't see any freedom riders. At the time, there was a lot of press in Britain about the American freedom riders in the South. The Beatles talked a lot about political and social movements. They were smart, even though they were practically adolescents. So young. Basically what people forget about them is that they were not dopey kids with guitars. They were from Liverpool, a tough city. They were tough, streetwise kids who knew their way around. Coming from Glasgow, a similar kind of city, there was an unspoken understanding between us. I never patronized them. A lot of the press used to speak to them in the beginning as though they were a bit dopey, but that soon changed when people realized just how quick they were.

I remember Lennon saying that they'd just done a new album. He was so excited about it, he said, "You know, Harry, what I like about it — there isn't a 'yeah, yeah, yeah' in it!" They were all happy they had taken a step forward in their music and would possibly be taken more seriously. I think John got his wish. He and Paul are arguably the most famous contemporary composers in the world. Their music is played by everyone from symphonies to western bands and has influenced subsequent generations of musicians as well.

On the plane there was talk about the American press and the press conference that was scheduled at Kennedy airport upon arrival. Brian Epstein worried about how they

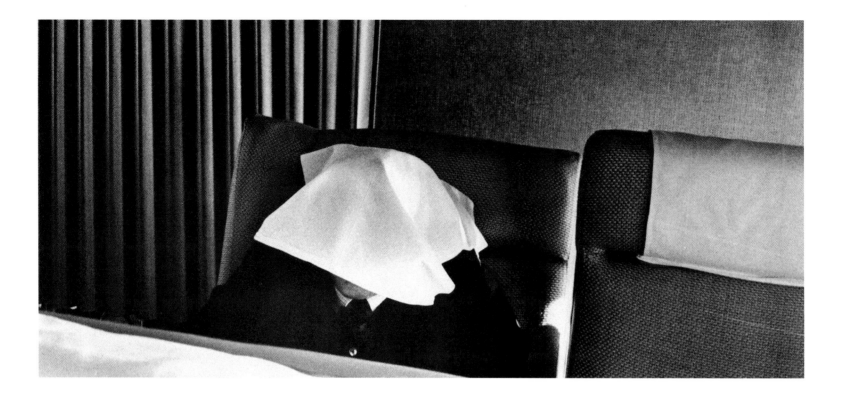

would do. He had heard a lot about the tough New York reporters. The closer we got, the more tension I could feel in the plane, although not among the Beatles themselves.

Where a few months before interest in them was lukewarm, with the sudden success of "I Want To Hold Your Hand," everybody in the U.S. wanted to talk to them, to meet them. Just a few days before we arrived, the Beatles had been featured on the cover of the U.S. edition of *Newsweek* magazine.

They all anticipated their first visit to America. They were excited. Before we landed, they started to wash up and seemed to be in good spirits. There was a naiveté about them, a playfulness that often emerged, like when Paul stuck his head out of the bathroom with his face covered in shaving cream. They liked to enjoy themselves, to have a good time, even when situations were tense or difficult. They were so young — none of the world-weariness had set in. This was their time.

WE LANDED AT KENNEDY AIRPORT at 1:20 PM on February 7, 1964. I was the fifth one off the plane. I had already told them what I wanted — for them to turn and wave to me going down the stairs with the big crowds of screaming fans in the background. They were briefed on what to do. But when they actually started off the plane, a lot of people in front of them and behind as well started shouting instructions, and they were beginning to forget what we had planned. I yelled and Ringo heard me in the melee and made them all turn around.

After "I Want to Hold Your Hand" hit number 1 on the American charts in February 1964, Capitol Records hired public relations people to work with Brian Epstein to organize the frenzy preceding the Beatles' arrival in America. Epstein had so much riding on how the Beatles would perform — not so much on the Ed Sullivan Show, he knew they could do that — but in front of the American press. He wanted them to live up to all of the advance expectations and anticipation created by the press agents.

The Beatles were taken to a small room at the airport for their first American press conference,

where they answered reporters' questions with quick-witted one liners. They were sensational. Americans thought they were — the American press expected — four dopey guys, which was their idea of Englishmen. But the Beatles could think on their feet and their quick wit won the Americans over right away. One of the first questions someone shouted was, "Are you guys for real?" To which John answered, "Sure, do you want to come up and have a feel?" They had everyone rolling

with laughter. They had the American press in the palm of their hands.

The advance publicity not only boosted record sales, it increased the general Beatlemania. The Ed Sullivan Show alone received over 50,000 requests for seats to the show. The theater would only seat around 700. Even Elvis Presley sent a telegram.

At Kennedy Airport, estimates ranged from 3,000 to 5,000 fans who waited to greet the Beatles. But they were kept away from the plane. There were only about 300 fans behind police barricades — the screaming girls with the welcome signs, some of them with the word Beatles misspelled. When I told my newspaper that all the fans had been held back from greeting the plane, I was told not to bother sending any pictures over to London. They were used to seeing mobs greet the Beatles all over Europe and they wanted nothing less. I didn't even bother to develop the film until about 12 years later. I just threw it in a bag in my closet. I'm glad I found and developed it. It was an historic day and I'm glad I documented it.

Sightseeing

BECAUSE GEORGE HARRISON was in bed with a sore throat, it was just John, Paul, and Ringo who visited Central Park in New York City. Their faces were youthful, happy, not jaded. Bright, open. Afterward when their lifestyles changed, they looked different.

In between giving radio interviews, rehearsing for the Ed Sullivan Show, and preparing for two concerts at Carnegie Hall, they found time to just play around.

While the three others were riding horse drawn carriages and clowning for photographers, George was sick in bed at the Plaza Hotel. George got a lot of get well telegrams at the hotel. Piled up on his lap, he was trying to read them all. He was wearing silk pajamas, a gift from someone, even though the pajamas were too small and the legs were way up to his kneecaps.

To get more light to take the picture, I had Andrew Fyall, the reporter for my newspaper, hold up the bedside lamp for me. You can see it floating off to the side in the photograph.

Radio talk show hosts would call up during the day to interview him and see how he felt. The radio station would say: "We're going *live* to George's sick bed." They brought up huge speakers and put them next to his bed so he could listen to the broadcast.

A girl sneaked up past hotel security and came into George's bedroom. She was quite attractive, too. I was in there at the time, along with a few other people, when she was lifted bodily by the security guard and carried out.

I told George that I wanted to stay in America, what a great place it would be to work in, and he said he couldn't imagine wanting to stay in America with all the plastic and phoniness. He used to criticize a lot and say that he was appalled by the brashness of the American people. George always used to call it plastic America. I think a lot of it was home-sickness.

Actually, I wanted to photograph them on the Brooklyn Bridge with the Manhattan skyline in the background, but it was an extremely cold day so we stayed close to the hotel. Ironically, I had to settle for Central Park with the West Side skyline and the Dakota apartment building in the background, where Lennon would later live and die.

To get onto the Beatles floor at the hotel, you had to get past two security guards. When we returned to the Plaza from our afternoon in Central Park, where the New York photographers had had their photo session with them, John, Paul, and Ringo stopped between the two guards on their floor.

I asked the American photographers what they thought of the Beatles. They told me they had seen everyone from Castro to royalty come and go and the Beatles had caused more commotion than most. They were right up there with the biggest celebrities of all time. These were the jaded New York press guys, the ones who wore their press cards in their hats — and even they were impressed.

After "I Want to Hold Your Hand" and "She Loves You" both became number one hits in the United Kingdom and the United States, the Beatles made rock and roll history in the U.S. by becoming the first artists to have the top five songs on *Billboard* magazine's top 100 hits: "I Want To Hold Your Hand," "Please Please Me," "Twist and Shout," "She Loves Me," and "Can't Buy Me Love." A phenomenal achievement. They also had three albums on the album chart at the same time: *Meet the Beatles*, *Introducing The Beatles*, and *With the Beatles*. *The Beatles Second Album* was released a few months later and became number one in less than a month.

Ed Sullivan

O
N THE PLANE TO NEW YORK they
kept saying, "We're going to meet Ed
Sullivan, Ed Sullivan." They were
all very reverent toward Ed Sullivan. It
was like seeing the Pope to them. They
always addressed him as Mister Sullivan. They knew just what Ed Sullivan
was doing for their career. The Beatles
were very excited, they wanted to be on
the Ed Sullivan Show.

We left the Plaza Hotel with swarms
of fans outside. The good-humored New
York City policemen were there trying
to keep order. "We see them!" cried the
girls outside as we rushed to the limo on
the way to the Ed Sullivan Show. The
fans had waited a long time outside in
the cold.

The five of us were crunched into
the back of the limo; it wasn't as big as
the limos are today. The girls rushed up
to the windows screaming, but it wasn't

scary. To see it from the Beatles perspective, to be at the center, was what I was there for.

Going off to the Ed Sullivan Show, they all gave each other support without saying anything. I think the fact that there were four of them kept them relatively normal. If there had been only one it would have been much harder to deal with all that was happening. Standing back looking at all their talent and new fame, one might be envious, but I really would not wish their life on anyone. They were isolated from everything because of the fans.

What's interesting about the Beatles is that this phenomenon had never happened before. Elvis and Sinatra had been idols in their day, but they were singers, they didn't compose their own music.

Ed Sullivan got the Beatles wig from someone in the audience and he put it on his head while warming up the crowd before the

show. It was estimated that over 73 million people watched the show, one of the largest TV audience ever.

When the Beatles began to sing, everyone in the audience started to yell. By now that had become the usual reaction and they expected it. It was almost impossible to hear them above the screaming and shouting.

The way they looked for the Ed Sullivan Show is a classic picture of the Beatles; it was the way America first saw them. This was how they used to dress all the time. Years later, Lennon said that he wished they had done like Mick Jagger and the Rolling Stones and just worn what they wanted.

When people see the onstage picture of the Beatles from the Ed Sullivan Show they ask, "Was this when they were still innocent?" They weren't really all that innocent, but they were very young. They came from Liverpool, which is a rough city. They used to talk about times when George got a black eye from being in fights. They had also been around the sleazy clubs in Hamburg before the first world tour, before all of the attention. They had hung around the red light district there during the very early days when they never knew if they were going to make it.

When we returned to the Plaza, the hotel was surrounded by fans again. The Beatles were virtual prisoners inside the

hotel. They wanted to do all sorts of things, like visit the Playboy Club, which was only a block away, but they couldn't get out of the hotel without being mobbed. They complained they were prisoners in their rooms. When I suggested combing their hair back and changing clothes so they could go unnoticed, they looked at me with amazement. They wouldn't hear of it.

After the show there was still the nervous tension from being on stage. They had to slow down and try to relax. Sometimes they would just collapse on the sofas in their suites and try to unwind, away from the loud confusion of the screaming fans.

A few days after the Sullivan show they took a train to Washington, D.C., in a blizzard to give a concert at the Washington Coliseum. The Beatles were excited by an invitation to a party at the British Embassy, but when they got there they were treated rudely by some of the guests. Later the British ambassador called to apologize for his guests' behavior.

Then it was back to New York for the concerts at Carnegie Hall before flying down to Miami a few days later to do another Sullivan show.

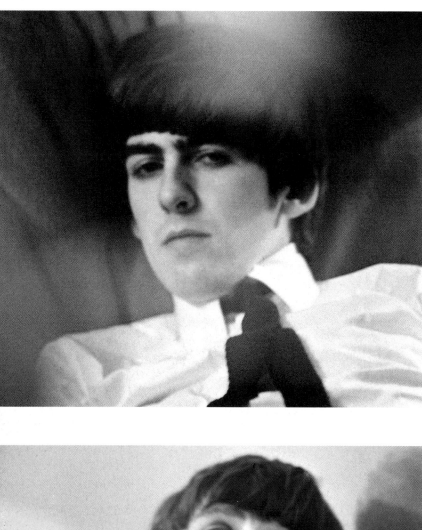

Miami

THE BEATLES CONTINUED on to Miami, where they were met at the airport by an estimated 7,000 hysterical fans. They were eager to do the Sullivan show a second time. The Beatles were always very deferential toward Ed Sullivan. They knew how important he was to their career.

I can still hear him in his distinctive voice introduce them as "Those nice young men from Liverpool." During rehearsals, they would say things like, "Mr. Sullivan, are we standing in the right place? Mr. Sullivan, do you want us to move over here?" They weren't saying "Take me or leave me, Mr. Sullivan." They ingratiated themselves with him as much as possible. They weren't the hang-loose, couldn't-care-less bunch who were giving amusing press conferences, which was the impression they always tried to give. In other words, they knew how and when to grovel when they felt they had to do it.

Actress Jill Hayworth with reporter David English (now Sir David English).

The Beatles being greeted by beauty contest winners.

At the airport, local beauty pageant winners met them coming off the plane and followed them wherever they went — even to the beach. To say that a lot of women were interested in meeting the Beatles would be an understatement.

Jill Hayworth, the actress, turned up in Miami to meet Paul. Her career was at its peak at the time; she had just starred in the film "Exodus" with Paul Newman.

In Florida the crowds were calm, very polite. The girls were shy and giggly, yet flirty. I wanted to photograph them on the beach and they obliged. The Beatles were all wearing the same thing. I think someone had sent over matching terry cloth cover-up outfits for them and they all put them on for a trip to the beach. With Ringo, the girls on the beach were polite, yet curious. You could never photograph like that now. A rock star of this magnitude would be mobbed today.

They rehearsed for the Sullivan show dressed very casually and wearing daft glasses. The dress rehearsal was taped before a live audience. They carefully checked everything, making certain that their equipment was in order for the performance. After all, it was live television and there was no time for retakes if anything went wrong. Their second appearance on the Ed Sullivan Show, broadcast from the Deauville Hotel, was watched by 75 million viewers, at the time, a record audience.

I left Miami to photograph Ian Fleming, the author of the James Bond books, at his home in Jamaica. When I told Mr. Fleming where I'd just come from, he and his wife wanted to know everything about the Beatles. The Flemings even had a complete collection of Beatles records there in Jamaica.

Cassius Clay

I N FLORIDA, the Beatles said they wanted to meet the world heavyweight champion Sonny Liston. This was before the famous Clay/Liston match. Liston told me that he didn't want to see the "bums" so I had to quickly substitute Cassius Clay. It was only later, after he beat Liston, that Clay changed his name to Muhammad Ali.

    We went down to the ring and Clay ordered the Beatles around telling them to lie down, line up, etc. He called Paul the pretty one, but told him,

"You're not as pretty as me." Clay was great. He was really smart. The Beatles were stunned when they walked out. They weren't happy because for the first time someone else had taken over. They had been acting really cocky and funny in their press conferences. They thought they were going to meet some dumb boxer and when they met Clay they were really thrown for a loop. They felt taken advantage of and wouldn't speak to me for a few days. Afterwards, Lennon said, "That man made a fool of us." It wasn't pleasant having the Beatles mad at me, especially Lennon.

Amsterdam and Copenhagen

T HE MESSAGE CAME OVER the wire service that Ringo was ill. I can't remember exactly, but I think it might have been his stomach again. There was speculation about whether or not their spring 1964 tour of Holland and Denmark would be cancelled. Everyone wondered how they would go on tour without him.

It didn't surprise me that one of them was ill. They used to be out all night every night in London. You'd hear about one or another of the Beatles dancing with movie stars or royalty at the Ad Lib Club in Soho or some other trendy spot. So it was no surprise Ringo was ill, he was probably exhausted.

Instead of cancelling they got Jimmy Nichol, another drummer, to stand in on the trip. He was a pleasant young man who was going to make the most of his days as a member of the most famous group in the world: he signed autographs and gave press interviews. Who could blame him? He was having a grand time.

If I remember correctly, John was pleasant to him, Paul was ambivalent, and George downright

didn't like him and thought he was a bit too pushy. They all agreed, Epstein included, that he was a very good drummer, not good-looking, but a good drummer. He was just a little guy who was lucky enough to fill in for Ringo on tour. A Beatle for a couple of days.

There were rumors that that was the end of Ringo, but when I saw Jimmy — no offense to him — I knew it wasn't so. Even though Lennon had once said, "When I feel my head start to swell, I just look at Ringo and know we're not supermen." The fans were disappointed that Ringo wasn't there. In the telephone office in Britain and in the General Post Office the operators had big blackboards which stated Ringo's condition up to the minute. They had so many thousands of calls about his health, they had to have extra switchboards put in in London.

Lennon didn't mind having Jimmy along at all, but the others were a bit wary of him. He was a bit older than the rest. I don't know any other time that they had to replace a member of the group because of illness. I had asked them to sit for a portrait with Jimmy Nichol and after I took it they scattered. Only John remained seated staring at the camera, still posing. This is typical of John, doing what he thought was the unexpected.

The Beatles gave two concerts in Copenhagen using Jimmy Nichol as their drummer before heading for Amsterdam, where they were scheduled to give a concert and appear live on Dutch TV.

The Beatles went for a boat ride around the canals in Holland before they did their show, just sight-seeing and greeting their fans. The bridges looked like they were straight out of a van Gogh painting. People jammed the bridges just to get a glimpse of the Beatles. Fans threw things off the bridges at their barge and jumped into the canals where the police had to pull them out. Police boats were with us for the entire ride.

It's the only time I can remember being with them when they actually went out to get a good look at a city. They really went sightseeing. The other times on tour, their lives would be spent slipping out of the hotel into a limousine and into a bar or club through the kitchen to avoid fans and then back out the same way to their hotel rooms late at night. The hotels became almost like prisons, where they were besieged by fans, unable to move about freely.

The Beatles gave a performance at the Blokker Exhibition Hall in Amsterdam the day after they appeared on a Dutch television show. In addition to the TV performance, they also gave

an interview and both segments aired a few days later.

Before the TV show, while John was getting his make-up, Paul clowned around with the make-up artist.

Later, John and George relaxed before the show, which was to be filmed before a live audience in a small studio.

The producers of the Dutch television show talked them into letting fans sit on the stage while they performed. They insisted it was safe, but what happened was that the producers arranged ahead of time to have the fans rush the stage at the conclusion of their performance, I guess to show the powerful effect the Beatles had on fans. Of course, it got a little bit out of hand. The fans rushed to the stage while the Beatles were still singing and chaos ensued. In the photo you can see how close the fans were and just a few seconds later, the pushing and shoving started and all hell broke loose. The equipment plugs got pulled out and John got punched in the back. The Beatles didn't like it at all and they never let anything like that happen again.

A Hard Day's Night

THIS PHOTOGRAPH WAS TAKEN during the filming of their first movie, "A Hard Day's Night" on the train used in the film. They changed the name of the film after Ringo came in one morning looking disheveled and hung over and said, "It's been a hard day's night."

When they were making the movie, people wondered what they'd be like in a film; they needn't have worried. The movie opened in July 1964 and was a smash hit. The critics said that although all four were good, Ringo was the most natural and was especially good.

I spent a couple of days traveling with them on the train from Paddington Station in London up to Crewe in the British Midlands and back again while they filmed. All of my friends wanted to know what they were like; even my mother and father were telling their friends who I was photographing. A few days on the set was enough for me — there were too many people and too much hysteria wherever they went. There was no way I wanted to cover them *all* the time.

Wilfred Bramwell, a British character actor who had a role in the film, was known for being a bit eccentric. I remember John saying, "I wish he would stop trying to kiss me."

Before each scene was called, the Beatles could often be found relaxing in the dining car.

Right
The film's director, Richard Lester, chats with John in one of the train compartments while Ringo reads the newspaper.

Below, right
Wilfred Bramwell, a British character actor, with John in the background.

Epilogue

T HE BEATLES WERE VERY OPEN about what they would let be photographed up until about '66 or '67. I didn't accompany them on their second world tour — I was away on other assignments at the time, but I joined them on their third world tour of America in the summer of 1966.

The Lennon remark about being more popular than Jesus plagued them and there were even some empty seats at the Shea Stadium concert. Their last stage performance was on August 29, 1966, in San Francisco. An era had ended.

Once they stopped touring, I didn't photograph them as a group anymore. When they got into that Sergeant Pepper's Lonely Hearts Club Band stage, they had clearly gone on to other lifestyles, and I went on as well.

During the time I was with them, I saw how they changed, how the fame affected them. They became more confident. They began to see themselves as extraordinary. Being a photographer, I didn't want to get too close. There were too many hangers-on by the end of the first world tour. As the Beatles changed and moved on, the people close to them often got hurt or left behind; their first wives, for one example, Pete Best for another. I just wanted to get photographs for the newspaper and then be on my way again.

Barbados Honeymoon

GEORGE MET PATTI BOYD on the set of "A Hard Day's Night." She was an extra in the movie and had a modeling career. When they married in 1966, where they had gone for their honeymoon was kept secret. With a bit of detective work, though, I tracked them to Barbados, where George had rented a house. I didn't know where they were staying, so I just went looking for them.

I had been looking all day and about 4:30 in the afternoon, on a quiet beach with beautiful sand, I decided to stop for a swim. Who should I see walking toward me but George. At first he thought it was a coincidence, but I explained why I'd come and promised to let him get on with his honeymoon if he'd let me take a few pictures first.

They were fine about it and we hung around together and had dinner that night. The people in Barbados were very polite and left them alone.

Later, when she married Eric Clapton, George said he was glad Patti married Clapton instead of some jerk.

WHEN THE BEATLES first started touring, there were no ground rules on what a rock concert was all about. Everything was new, no one knew what would happen next. By the third world tour, we knew what to expect.

It was 1966 and the *Rubber Soul* album was going to the top of the charts. The Beatles recorded "Yellow Submarine," "Paperback Writer," and "Eleanor Rigby." The album *Revolver* was released and John Lennon spent part of the year filming *How I Won the War*.

By the time the third world tour began, the Beatles were wearing pin-striped suits instead of only the dark solid-colored ones — but they all still dressed alike. The Rolling Stones had recently come into celebrity and dressed anyway they liked. It wasn't too long after that that the Beatles started dressing individually, too.

They toured Memphis, Chicago, Cincinnati, St. Louis, New York, Washington, D.C., Toronto, and San Francisco, among others, and also traveled to Japan and the Philippines.

During the tours, they often rested backstage on mattresses or pallets on the floor. They would

sit there and tune guitars, getting ready for their performance. They used to like looking in a mirror before going on and shaking their heads like Saint Bernards coming out of the water to get their hair just right. Fluffy. So the bangs would fall just right.

Onstage, things hadn't changed too much — they were still bowing from the waist and they still loved to perform. The minute they opened their mouths, the frenzy and screaming would start. They couldn't hear anything so after a while they started improvising and singing anything that came into their heads. It didn't matter what they sang — no one could

hear them anyway. They just made a joke of it, playing around, having fun.

They generated mass hysteria everywhere they went. All the young faces, hysterically crying, screaming, out of control, not exactly knowing why. Thinking back, the crowds were really quite well-behaved in comparison to what they are like now. Loud, but well-behaved. Quite well dressed. Middle class. Very few black kids in the audience. Yet the Beatles respected black music very much. They have said that their very early influences were people like Chuck Berry and Little Richard.

The Beatles were starting to worry about people throwing things on to the stage from the audience. John and Paul had both been hit by coins, shoes, etc. They were getting hurt by them. Off stage, the Beatles were beginning to tire of the madness of touring.

They gave their last concert in Candlestick Park in San Francisco in 1966.

Chicago

LENNON GAVE AN INTERVIEW to English journalist Maureen Cleave, in which he said that the Beatles were more popular than Jesus. It caused quite an uproar. I was somewhere else on another story and was told to get to Chicago, where the Beatles were, as quick as I could. Lennon was very upset and started to actually sob, saying, "Why did I open my big mouth, why did I do it? I didn't mean it." And the rest of the Beatles were really quite annoyed with him. He issued a formal apology retracting his statement.

People in the Bible belt were burning Beatles records. It was a very serious thing; people were calling radio talk shows condemning the Beatles. Record stores in the Bible belt of America were refusing to sell their records and D.J.'s across the country were keeping count of the number of record stores that refused to sell their records and announcing the results on the air. This went on for weeks. At a concert in Chicago, the police lined up in front of the stage to protect the Beatles from threats from outraged fans. Even a later concert at Shea Stadium wasn't sold out because of it — about 10,000 seats were left empty.

At the time Lennon was not cocky about it although he was later. Of course, some people think he was right.

Press conference

BRIAN EPSTEIN waits for the Beatles to go on at Shea Stadium, August 15, 1965, while George tries to relax before the show.

At press conferences in 1966 (Memphis, right), if someone asked a smart-ass question, the Beatles would put them in their place. It was a mistake to ask something like "Do you have any conscience about corrupting the youth of America?" because they always had a quick retort. No one asked them that kind of question twice.

Ringo Starr

RINGO WAS NOT sophisticated at all at first. You can see in some of the pictures that Ringo really defers to John and Paul.

I remember asking Duke Ellington once who was the most important person in a band and he said definitely the drummer. A bad drummer can throw off the rest of the band. Ellington said he didn't care who he had, it could be the man in the moon, as long as he could drum. Everything comes from that. Ringo was not the man in the moon, he was a street-wise kid from Liverpool who could drum. He was rough around the edges, but he learned quickly.

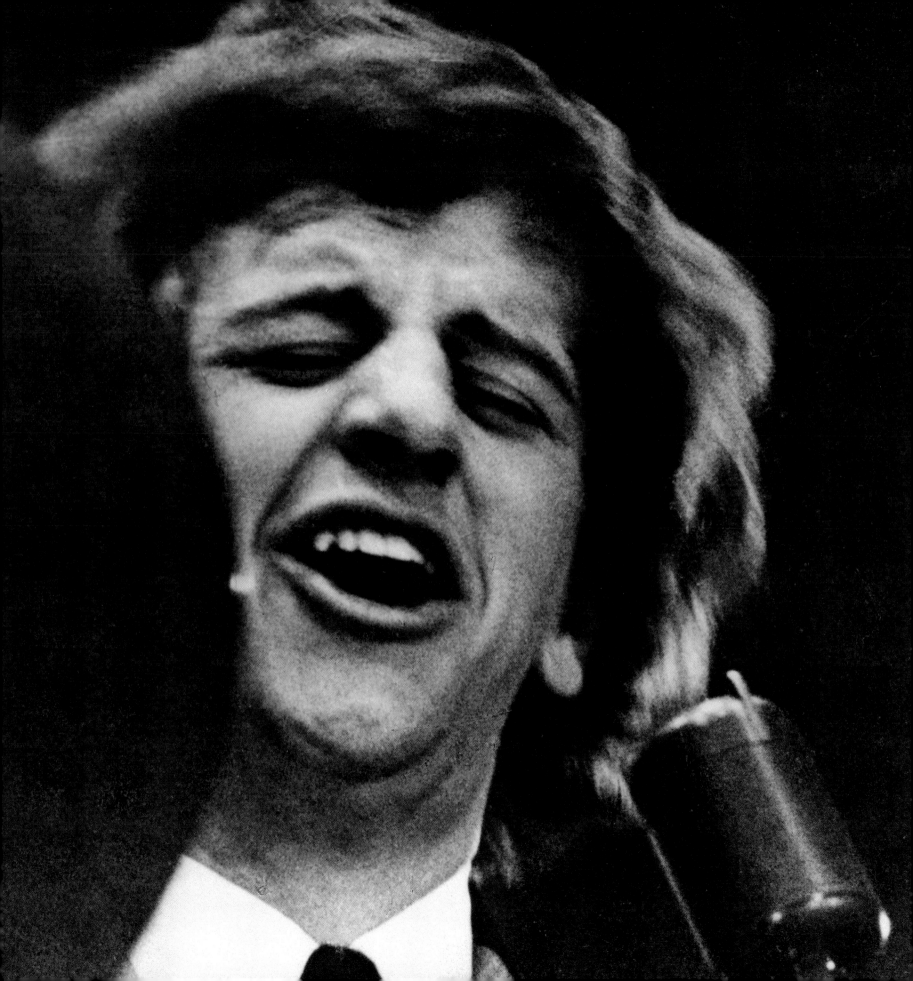

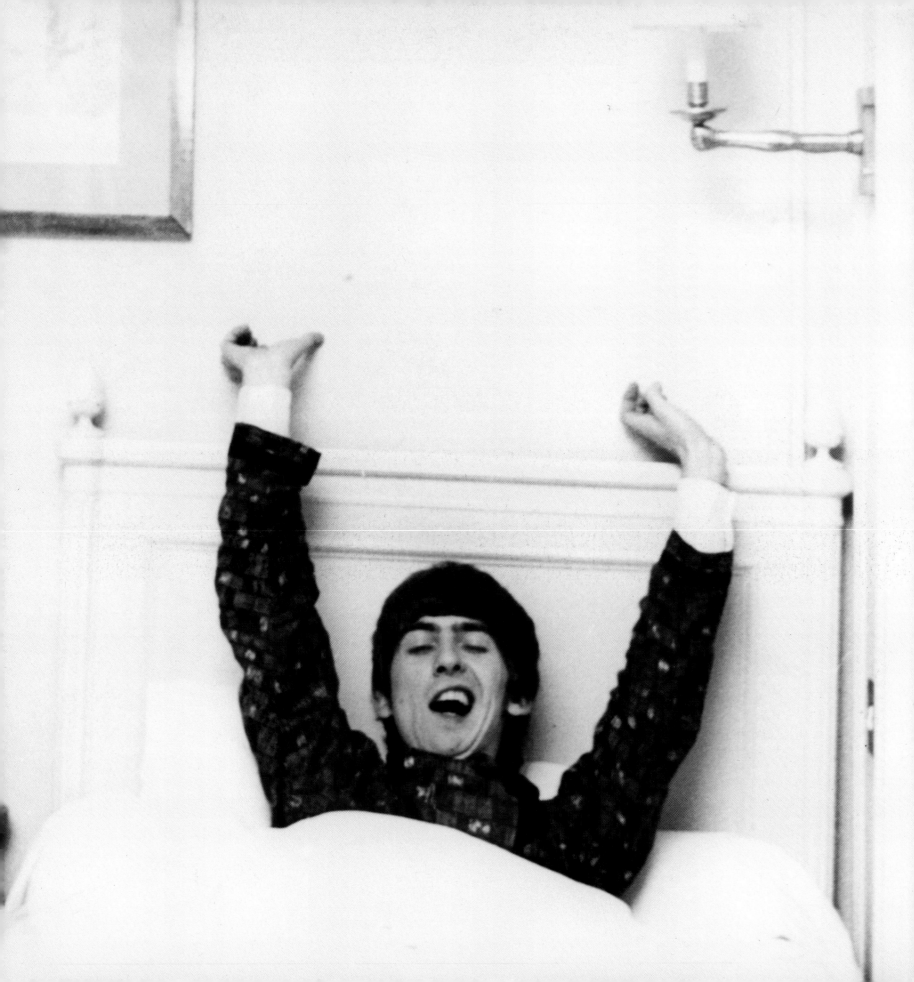

George Harrison

I WAS ACTUALLY CLOSER to George than to the other three. We went out to clubs sometimes and I always sat and talked with George much more than I did with the others. Lennon used to talk about intellectuals he had met; Paul liked to talk about the movie stars he'd met; and Ringo about the royalty who had come to meet them. George talked about Segovia, the great Spanish guitarist. "I'll never be as great as he is," he said, "but that's what I'm aiming for."

It's interesting that the one song on the *Rubber Soul* album written by George was titled "Think for Yourself." He was quietly determined to keep his integrity.

Paul McCartney

To me, Paul was the leader of the Beatles. Paul was also the kindest one. He would always find time to talk to the fans, the reporters, whoever. He would make people laugh. He would stop and talk and sign autographs. He would always be the last to leave. If there was a decision to be made John looked to Paul for confirmation. Decisions were definitely made between the two of them — although they took pains not to show the outside world that the two of them were in charge.

John Lennon

THE LAST TIME I saw John alive was from a distance at an anti–Vietnam War peace rally in Bryant Park in New York City in the late sixties, where he said, "All we're saying is give peace a chance." And I thought to myself, 'He's in trouble.' It's alright as long as you protest in your own country, but Lennon was in America, not Britain. I knew the State Department would try to deport him because of what he was saying — and he'd been up on a drug charge in 1968, too. He did all he could to stay here and eventually it was alright, but it was very, very close.